MW00748042

The Beast that God has Kissed

To Henry Bailey,
who taught me the language
with which men speak to beasts

A special thank you to
George Beith, Eric Moore,
and, of course,
Rhonda

Acknowledgements

Some of these poems have appeared previously in *Directions, HighGrader Magazine,* and *The Manitoulin Recorder;* others have been read on the CBC Radio program "Out Front," and the CBC Northern Ontario Radio programs "Morning North" and "Points North."

The Beast that God has Kissed

Songs from the Birch Lake Road

by
Charlie Smith

Your Scrivener Press

Copyright © the Author, 2000

No part of this book may be reproduced or transmitted in any
form by any means, except for brief passages quoted by a
reviewer, without written permission from the publisher — or,
in the case of photocopying, a license from the Canadian
Copyright Licensing Agency.

Canadian Cataloguing in Publication Data

Smith, Charlie, 1948-
    The beast that God has kissed: songs from the Birch Lake
    Road

ISBN 1-896350-10-0

1. Country life — Ontario, Northern — Poetry. 2. Ontario,
Northern — Poetry. I. Title

PS8587.M5242B43 2000   C811'.6   C00-932885-8
PR9199.3.S64B43 2000

Book design: Laurence Steven
Cover design: Chris Evans
Back cover photo of Charlie Smith, courtesy of Ron Erwin

Published by *Your Scrivener Press*
465 Loach's Road,
Sudbury, Ontario, Canada, P3E 2R2
scrivener@sympatico.ca
www3.sympatico.ca/scrivener

Table of Contents

Hunting

Spirit

Character

The Line in the Sand

Preface

Charlie Smith's poems are limited in place to the low lying bush country outside of Massey, Ontario. It's landscape that hardly seems to rank in relation to the poetic grandeur of T.S. Eliot's London or Robert Service's Yukon. And the voices that speak from this landscape come from a seemingly unimpressive and overlooked pedigree — tractor operators trying to nurse life from scraggy cattle farms; blue collar men sitting with a bottle of rye and a reservoir of bullshit around a campfire after the kill. This is the terrain of Charlie Smith. But with this, his first book of poetry, he has proven himself to be one of Canada's most original and provocative poetic voices.

On a technical level alone, the poems are magnificent. Smith adopts the simple stand-by of the rhyming verse; there is nothing experimental or cutting edge about the form. There doesn't need to be. With beguiling simplicity, Smith uses his poems to tell stories. His use of meter and rhyme appear so effortless that the reader is drawn in beyond the words of the page. The reader becomes a confidant, a participant in an intimate and profound conversation.

And it is the conversation that sets Charlie Smith apart from the pack. There are poems of tenderness — for both love and the land. But beneath most of Smith's poetry is the articulation of the struggle rural men face as they try to hold their own in a culture that has relegated them to the backshed of history. And Charlie is not about to go peacefully. He emerges as one of the few voices on the Canadian scene that defiantly explores the raw edges of class and cultural conflict between rural and urban Canada.

The ravens cheer and guide us
And the new men hate out way,
With our coats of fibre fire
At the closing of the day.

Smith kicks in the door of the urban-created notion of wilderness as a tame and gentle Cathedral. He champions men who enjoy driving fast on backroads, with a two-four of beer and a rifle loaded for the fall hunt. In the hands of a lesser poet the sentiments might appear jingoistic or ugly, but Smith manages to elevate these characters and their experiences: he shows us men who remain deeply imbued with the primeval forces of nature.

We are technologic predators
Singing songs as old as time,
As we join the waltz of winter
When the horned one's in his prime.

It's provocative and unsettling writing. Perhaps mostly because in Canada we have grown used to a domesticated rural voice made safe for prime time consumption. Charlie Smith refuses to be quaint. Like the Highland Scots at the time of the clearances, or the remnants of the Dakota Sioux seeking sanctuary in Saskatchewan, Smith's rural Canadians are fighting for a way of life that is disappearing. They are people well aware that their culture is being hemmed in. They have no place in the new vision of the land — a vision that renders the frontier a safer but impotent place.

You are taking my life, one law at a time,
You, and your rules of today . . .
There's no Medicine Line I can cross to escape,
As you legislate my life away.

So what does this offer the reader who does not live on the northern landscape? What does it say to a reader who does not hunt or raise cattle, or love to drive too fast on country roads? A great deal. Charlie Smith reminds us that in a supposedly global world, the most powerful stories are still told by voices rooted in a particular landscape and culture. His poetry is a powerful testament to the compelling but threatened culture of northern Ontario. Smith doesn't write to please. But take a walk with him along the gravel ruts of the Birch Lake Road. You just might learn to see the land in a way you never imagined.

— Charlie Angus, Editor
HighGrader Magazine

Farming

BIRCH LAKE

It's not the gravel grabs me,
When I hit the Birch Lake Road;
It's not the leaving pavement,
Or the way the pace is slowed —

It's the rocks, I guess, and tucked in fields,
And the hills, and bush and men,
Who live along the Birch Lake routes,
When I am home again.

It's knowing every dog by name,
And all the herds by sight;
It's hearing, knowing in the dark,
Who's howling in the night.

I was shook around this continent,
Like a pebble in a can;
But I'm rooted here in the Birch Lake hills,
And I'm a Birch Lake man.

I'm a Birch Lake farmer,
It is all I want to be;
So the rattling ruts of the gravel roads —
They feel like home to me.

RUNOFF

Water through snow, when it runs in the spring
Is attractive to children as near anything,
And I have to admit, if asked, "Is it fun?"
That even I like to make spring water run;
So I dig out the culvert under the lane,
Then next year I figure I'll do it again.

I was knee-deep in March, wet slush and pleasure,
I would shovel a bit, then watch at my leisure —
The water was running: giggling snow
Soaked in the slush, then slobbering slow
Seeping along over grass from last year,
Then sucked in the culvert and foaming like beer.

My gray house with its history was dreaming above
Of long, lilting lifetimes of labor and love,
For the land where I'm steward, was farmed here before —
How many farmers have smiled at this chore?
For the earth, wind and water will seep in your soul,
And this is one rite that ties up the whole.

My son and a friend, when driving by greet me.
I wave back at them, but they're not going to cheat me;
It's just once a year, and those two teenage boys
Can go off and play with their more modern toys.
But when they came back (I was dry in my home)
They asked, "Where is Brandon?" — but I was alone.

"Then who was the child who was helping you there,
With his feet in the water, with wind in his hair?
He puddled in puddles, and trenched with his toe."
They both clearly saw him — I really don't know;

A lost little ghost from the house on the hill?
I didn't see him (I did feel a thrill);

And I did feel a presence a couple of times
Like the long shivered tinkle of distant wind chimes . . .
Water through snow when it runs in the spring
Is attractive to children as near anything:
The earth, wind and water will seep in your soul,
And this is one rite that ties up the whole.

CHUCK, LEAVING HOME

Did you hear it?
Just as my brother's car bore you down the lane
The whole farm, sleepy with fog,
Shrugged languidly — pregnant green,
Decked with blossoms like a spring bride
Moist with passion, demon lover —
Clung to me, sucking my life into hers.

Earthfast groaned.

The hay along the driveway curled towards the wheels;
An apple tree, young and lustful, waved branches past your
    face;
Dandelion fluff caught in the grill,
And fog rolled heavy in from the hilly fields,
Gray green and thick, obscuring,
Until the car was out of sight.

The dew condensed on plow, on leaf and flowers,
Formed to droplets on the shining parts,
And slid like tears
Upon the windows of our home.

DAWN POEM

The bobolink sits on the gnarled lilac tree
And claims to the world, this is his!
From the big shingled house to the pole by the drive,
And I guess if he holds it, it is.
If he proclaims it in story and song
And fights in the air, if he must,
And wakes up the farmer, still sleeping at six,
And sings like he's ready to bust.
The tomcat's still sluggish; he's hunched by the queen;
He's no time to think on the bird.
And the bull's in the barnyard to hide from the flies;
I'm doubting that he's even heard.
The yard dog lies high on the cool concrete step,
He can see all his world with one eye;
And all of us hold what we can in the green —
We hold, or we're willing to try.
We all share this range, in this moment of time
When June comes up tawny and red;
But only the bobolink does it so proud —
And sings like he's waking the dead.

FLOWER SEA

Into the sea of flowers
I go like fate unleashed;
The smoky steel, the whirling reel,
The roaring big red beast.
The chatter of the knife on guards,
The air turns sweet and green;
In order laid, where beauty played,
It's hay where I have been.
It's hay to the horizon,
Around, around, around;
Before the sun, till day is done,
I lay it on the ground.
It's bales like sleeping bison,
It's windrows straight and true,
And I'm in the sea of flowers . . .
I love the job I do.
The dawn as cool as perfumed ice,
The noon as hot as coal,
Then shadows race the baler's pace
Where the waves of flowers roll.
Go fishing in your sideroad trucks,
Go to your camp by car;
I'd rather hay than go and play —
I'd rather hay, by far.
I'm in this sea of flowers,
In the beauty going round,
Intoxicated by the scent,
And the rolling of the ground.
Lulled by the heat and motion,
Laved by the sweat and dew,
Loving every moment,
Longing for more to do.

HAY GULLS

Hawk! Hawk!
The hundred gulls lift off as one
With quadrilles wheeling in the sun;
Light and shadow on the wing,
Confusing to the eye and mind . . .
And the hawk is hunting other kind —
Not these incongruous lakers.

Rain? Rain?
Discussing the probability,
They land behind the haybine's lee,
Feasting on the flotsam.
My companions all day long
Behind a snatch of shanty song:
The lake crowd in the hayfield.

Here! Here!
The scouts have found me; they always do,
Almost before the backswath's through;
Circles conducted in the sky —
As pilot fish pursue the shark,
They shadow me till close to dark
Then cool themselves in Huron.

Wet. Wet.
The water must feel awful nice,
To float and digest all those mice
And insects in the evening.
Do they dream fields of fresh-mown hay,
And of following me, the long hot day,
As I dream their cool shadows?

OTHER FARMERS

Sometimes, you know, I just know things,
Like when noon rolls around . . .
It can be cloudy, no hint there —
Say, I'm down plowing ground;
Suppose, I'm in a different place,
On unfamiliar land —
I usually can tell right off
Just where due north would stand.
Hell, I can spot another farmer
Clean across a street,
Even if he's dressed up nice
And I never heard him speak.
'Cause he can tell the time of day
Without, he sees a clock;
And he can cover rougher ground —
You can see it in his walk.
He knows the cycles, how beasts speak,
And what he tries he can;
Among the fops, the fools, the folks,
He shines out as a man.
He seems to have a "way" with him,
A sort of grimy shine,
As if the God of growing things
Has marked him: "This one's mine!"

FIELD WRITING

I   TAG ALDER FIELD

The tag alders clawed at the edge of the field
And advanced imperceptibly fast.
The spruce set pickets up here, and there,
Determined: reconquer at last!
The poplars and pine, they are officer kind
And lead from the back of the row;
But they're marching out now through the dead furrow trench
And nothing of value can grow.
Little is left of the kingdom of man,
A man with a hand like rough pine
Who had thrown back the foe with his axe and his hoe
And bragged to his wife, "This is mine."
I'll bet that he probably wore out a team
Till the strength of his body was past;
But he carved sixty acres out of the bush,
And he probably thought it would last.
You can follow his furrows, clean up to the rock,
And each is as straight as a die;
But there isn't a half left of what he had cleared —
Had he lived, he'd be wondering why.
His buildings are down; it's a shame in a way —
It's a damn bloody tragedy too!
But lumber is mortal, near bad as a man,
And nails die a natural death too.
But the land, that's the worst; it's an eternal trust
That you get when they hand you your deed;
And some things are sacred and should be beyond
The rules of profit and greed.

II RESURRECTION

I am writing a poem in the taggy old field:
Turn down the alders and grin —
When was the last time it sang of its yield?
The spruce whisper, "Long has it bin;
Long as a lifetime, long as a log,
Many a winter did nest."
But I plow down the poplar, the chokecherry bush,
The whispering spruce and the rest.
I find the old furrows and strike out anew;
I sing to the red diesel roar,
And the field heaves her bosom and flexes her arms,
And the sod on the mull-boards says, "More!"
I am writing a poem and my black lines are straight,
A rhyme that a dead man can see;
And he circles the edges just out of my sight,
And he whispers "Oh, thank you!" to me;
"Long was she fallow and ruin, my love,
Long lay my pretty, despair."
He reflects on my mull-boards each time I go round —
You can't see him quite, but he's there.
I am the savior of land gone to brush;
I am the rod and the way.
And of all of the poems I've written so far —
The plow wrote my favourite today.

PURSUED

I'm tired of driving this bleeding beast
Around the endless rows of hay,
Racing shadows from the bush
Damp at the end of day.

The poor thing's hot, but so am I,
Though I have no gauge to show;
Around, around the hammers sound
Steady, sad and slow.

I'm sick of being always broke,
I'm sick of sun and air,
And my ass is sore from riding days
Upon this black backed chair.

This poor old tractor's past its prime,
Too many hours show;
And I guess those hours tell on me —
Around, around I go.

I don't want no easy life,
I don't ask the sky;
But decent prices, new machines,
Would do, before I die.

JOHNSON'S FLAT

That farm killed him —
As sure as a gun to his head.
The terrible fertility of it.
He bought it from the Widow Johnson
(There should have been a hint in that);
Flat bottomland it was, Black Muck.
Johnson had tilled it — that job killed him.
It wouldn't hold a crop,
Not long.
But oh God, it produced
Three, four crops a year:
A barn buster.
A man breaker.
Fence posts popped out of that ground,
Black willows flourished in the ditches,
And it was always a fight;
Plowing was a muddy bitch:
Always a third of it
Lying turned and black and wanton.
And oh, the grain . . .
The truck scurried to the combine
Groaning under the load,
Stuck, five, six times a day.
He was young and plump, ambitious . . .
It broke him, that farm:
His back, his hands, and farmer's lung;
His hearing went from the tractor blast,
And by fifty he was dead.
And that fat farm —
Fertile whore — just smiled and said "Next!"

LEACH LAND

A good man that!
The second of that type
I've seen pour out his strength into that place:
Buck up the square shoulder on the endless wheel
Of the seasons,
And hold their sunburned noses to that clay ground;
Uphill on the hills — against the flow of economics —
Pressed into the wind . . .
The never ending wind.

Open your strong veins, by God,
And pour your lifeblood in that fertile land —
The second of that type;
Broken just next door.

I'd rather let it flow by me, grow by me,
Over me, a bit by bit dog paddle with life;
No striking out strong for me,
No wrestling with angels,
No lying in bed with hoses in me . . .
A midday nap is more my style;
I'd rather bend, than break
Like good men do.

THE TOUR

Here you go up to the blueberry hill
Where Bob Johnston built by the hollow.
The driveway's still there, just off to the left;
It's rough; if you're wanting to follow
You best put this rig into its four-wheel drive —
Go slow, see, the culvert's washed out.
The water came down one May in the spring
And pushed poor Bob Johnston about.
It flooded the fields that you see over there,
The ones with the red gads and brush;
It washed out the dam that he had by the rock —
Slow down, look around, there's no rush.

See Bob had planted in April that year,
His oats were as high as your shin;
And farming don't pay in rough country like this,
But Bob had begun to begin.
It drowned his three sows in that ramshackle shed,
It carried his rail fence away;
So he sat in his house, see the footing's up there,
And he brooded and pondered all day.
Then he emptied the fuel from his one coal oil lamp,
And he spread kerosene on the floor;
And where he went then, after he struck that match,
I don't know, but he ain't here no more.

Still, if you have the money, the place is for sale,
Like the sign by the road told you so;
You seem like a nice young fella to me,
Just take all your dreams, off you go.
I know that you see this place in your mind
With a nice rustic cabin up there,
And maybe some chickens out here by the drive . . .

An orchard: apple and pear —
Some cows in the barn, a horse or a team,
A tractor, machinery and swine . . .
I know what you're thinking, don't look so surprised,
It's the same dream, Bob Johnson's and mine.

OH

Somewhere in the darkened yard
A hound mouthed soft vowels,
Each single syllable note as clear and pure
As a thousand years of blood can sing.
No foreign scent had sparked that voice
And added break or bray;
No hunger, thirst, or bitch in heat
Had quested forth that song to give it bell and ring;
No prey to chase with hungry hope had harshed it out
To bellow, bark and yelp —
But just the summer soft and singing night,
With west wind whispers round the ears,
And half a moon so neat and clean,
And the familiar warmth of all the farm:
The cattle sleeping on the grass,
The drifting sweetness of the hay,
The coziness of here at home.
And all of that was in the song,
And each note was a perfect poem . . .
A lullaby to lull me off
And lay me easy in my dreams
Of everything he sings.

AUGUST

August is pressing in: weeds in the ditches,
Dangling bushes with berries, the bitch's
Round riping fruit on the trees there to tempt . . .
Get thee behind me! I am exempt.
The trefoil's past cutting, but I am still haying,
There are seedpods and browning, it murmurs of staying;
The grain's turning yellow like dye in her hair —
It's tempting the combine, like I didn't care.
The cattle are plump, though the pasture is dry,
But there's promise of storm in the dark henna sky.
There's a blush in the cloud and a dust on the hill —
Oh August, you vixen, you give me a thrill.
I'd lie down beside you and curve to your breast
And the red beast I'm driving *is* pleading for rest . . .
I am racing the shadows on the long endless row,
And August is whispering, "Give in, let it go."
August caresses my hair with sweet hands,
And her breath is the scent of the soul of the land.

MOON FOG

Don't tell me the moon has nothing to do with it:
Not when it's shining down
At half past summer,
Not when the dew lies so heavy on the world
That it would be frost at another time,
Say, one more revolution.
Even the trees can feel it in them,
Pulling branches till the leaves are inside out,
Sucking at the air, gulping it in,
Feeding on it in the gloom,
Basking in the moonlight.
The cut fields enfold it too:
It crawls along the edges of the hills
As rivers of fog;
It soaks your shirt, your hair, your fur
And lies across your shoulder
Like a cool arm.
The predators are hunting, the prey is out,
The world is pulling the dampness over her
Like a blanket in the moon —
Fruit and feed, copulate and nurse the young,
Reach down hard into the soil . . .
There's moon fog in the gullies.

CRABAPPLES
circa 1800 to 2100

The crabapple grows on the edge of the ridge
Where the wind blows a little less cold;
And it thrives 'mong the cherry, the maple and ash —
All glory in crimson and gold.
And oh it was pleasant on warm autumn days
To sway on the wind from the south,
And clear the new field and go back to the house
With a crabapple popped in your mouth.
The sky was as blue as a rich uncle's shirt
Comin' up on the road through the farm,
And the gray weathered buildings made a display
To enhance the wild apple tree's charm.
The town's grown a little just over the ridge
And there's new houses pressin' each side,
But the crabapples stand in prominent view
'Mong the landscaping trained to the tide.
There's weeds in the gardens and doors hanging free
And game for the larder and eye,
And it's pleasant in autumn on warm afternoons
Pickin' crabapples for pie —
Pickin' crabapples to put them away,
For jelly and crabapple wine.
Sit in the tree as the dusk settles down
And hope that the buck is on time.
Walk round the bush with your pack and your bow
Into the fragrant south breeze,
Munchin' crabapples and puttin' it on,
Gathering up for the freeze.

HARVEST RAIN

The clouds are black in the north-northwest,
Raised like an angry fist;
And they roil like oil on horizons dark:
Crags cry — lightning kissed.
Here on the field the air is still
And the combine chatters and groans;
I avert my eyes from the threatening skies
Where thunder growls and moans.
I crawl like a mouse among the stocks
And reap the ripe heads in;
I rape the world I created here
And shatter it in the bin.
But I'm just a dot, in this sweeping spot,
A moving target true;
And I've acres to harvest before it rains,
And that's what I will do.
The setting sun has made its run
To the black in the north-northwest;
I've spoken charms from the broken harms
And I haven't time to rest.
If the old girl holds together till dark
And the dew and the rain don't come,
Or the lightning fry me in my seat,
I maybe might get done.
I maybe might, but the air gets bright,
And a fresh damp wind sweeps down;
I avert my mind, as from shameful times,
And I watch the reels go round.
I watch the reels and the muddy wheels —
Can I keep the rain at bay?
And keep the thought in a sacred spot:
Dare I stretch the day?
If I had words of power to speak,

Or the faith of a mustard seed,
Would they not be worsted, wasted here
On such a minor greed?
And if all of us wished on the weather we want,
What a wild scrap that would be.
So I simply smile, and head for the tarp
When the first sharp drops strike me.

OVERCOMPENSATION

I called for the rain, in anger and pain;
I scratched terrible runes in the dust.
I called to the moon, the gull, and the loon . . .
Now everything's mould, mud, and rust.
My hay that was stunted, is tall and uncut,
The pasture is getting ahead,
There are mushrooms galore in the gloom of my yard,
Fairy rings yellow and red.
There are big croaking frogs, that splash in the stream
(That I cynically still call my lane),
And the thunder god's dance, given any good chance,
It's drizzle, or downpour, then rain.
The haybine is hooked and it squats in the yard,
I've overhauled everything, twice.
I know we need rain, as we also need sun,
But a bit of dispersal'd be nice.
It's been two weeks of wet after one month of drought —
I take the joke good as I can;
But I find myself shouting as new clouds roll up:
"Come down and fight like a man!"

BILLY BUCK

He pulled in the yard in a fifty-six
Five ton Chevy truck.
He had cattle racks; on the rusty door
His name read Billy Buck.
A cheap cigar was in his mouth,
And dollars in his eyes,
And his voice was polished everyday
From telling fancy lies.
He clomped on the porch, "Hello, this place!"
And he knocked on the old screen door;
Invited in, he pulled his boots
Off, for the polished floor.
"Good day," he said, "I'm Billy Buck.
Is this the Peever Place?
I heard about you clean from town!"
A smile was on his face.
Now, Old Man Jones, he lit his pipe
And said how that was true;
"I heard about the cattle man.
I guess now, that is you."
"Oh, how they talk! But pay no mind —
I'm just a businessman.
I'll trade and buy most anything,
Or sell it if I can."
The old man smiled a weary smile
Like old fields in the sun,
And on that face was every trace
Of all the things he'd done;
And everything was rich and right,
And each thing in its place;
The stamp of God was on the man,
And wisdom in the face.
"I ain't got any stock to speak,

No money left to spend,
But I put the coffee on the stove,
So have a cup my friend.
Then tell me why you came this way
And tell me what you know;
We'll gab a bit and have a sit —
Don't talk of trading though."
"Well," Bill, he says, "Now, Mr. Jones
I have heard this marvelous thing
From every second farm around,
'Bout how you pick and sing.
I'd kinda like to hear ya,
'Cause folks all say I should —
And it would be a pleasure
If you were half that good.
The old man took his banjo down
And stroked each throbbing string;
The music ran like rivers rush —
Then he began to sing.
His voice it flowed like wind or wheat,
Like rain at haying time;
Each word was rich in meaning,
Each meaning had a rhyme.
Billy's eyes grew glazed as glass,
He leaned back in the chair;
The music sort of picked him up,
Then sat him down somewhere.
The banjo notes ran in his blood,
His skin crawled on his frame;
And Billy Buck forgot the thing
That echoed in his name . . .
And Billy he went swinging back
To when he was a boy;
He remembered things that he had lost,
His face was rapt with joy.

Then the banjo singer let him go
But the world seemed fresh and bright;
And Billy's face it seemed to glow
With some eternal light.
He sat in silence for awhile
With a tear up in his eye;
Then he said, "For once they told the truth —
For once they didn't lie.
They said you sang like angels,
And I swear they were not wrong.
There's a heifer cow in my truck right there . . .
You just bought her for a song."

CHEEK TO JOWL

Men and beasts, we were together
Cheek to jowl,
Voice to growl;
And men were men, by God,
With God,
And beasts were as they were.
We made no pretensions then —
We had dominion over
Beasts of the field and fowls of air
And fish of the sea.
Stewards of the soil we were,
In a terrible harmony:
Feed and tend and love and kill,
Then eat the flesh, of what you drew
Mewling on a winter morn
Out of life and into life.
We were minions then of nature:
Lords of the seasons,
Kings upon our farms.
We knew the smell of life and death,
And on our breath
Was the taste of our mortality.

CATTLE DOG

Pudge was just a half grown pup
When I took her off the chain;
She was sitting in a junk yard lot —
I could see she had a brain.
And no one had to tell me;
She spoke right to my heart.
I said, "Sure! I'll make a dog of this,
And she will do her part."
Her mother was a Shepherd,
And her pa, a travelin' man
(A corgi someone told me,
But I can't swear, off hand).

But Pudge, she was a doer,
Handled cattle from the start.
And I never had to yell at Pudge;
She read me from the heart.
She would deal with wrangy cattle,
Fight a mean bull, face to face,
And I could leave contented
Knowing Pudge would watch the place.
Her eyes would look right at you,
Like she read your deepest thought;
And she sent pictures in my sleep,
If trouble hit the lot.

She got old and stiff, on duty,
Fighting wolves, and bears, and coon,
Having pups and watching cattle,
In the long cold winter moons.
She was worth two men, or maybe more,
And I loved her like a friend,
But her life was in her duty,

And they caught her in the end.
And they bore her down and broke her —
Thought I'd see what the vet could do.
Brave as a bear, she staggered in —
I told her, "That will do!"

And God, it broke my hard old heart,
When I left her there behind.
But there was hope, I kinda thought —
Her eyes looked in my mind.
They put her down on the table,
And I wrapped her in my coat,
And I buried her on the windbreak hill,
And I knew my heart was broke.
I shed hot tears, and I spoke to God,
By the planted pines, I stood.
I said, "Only men have souls, I guess.
But check, 'cause this dog should."
Now don't you laugh, but I carved a stone:
"Pudge, good girl!" it said.
I chiseled it in rough field staff,
And I placed it by her head.

Pudge's name's still magic
With the cattle and the kind,
And it still holds weight with me, my boy,
'Cause she melded with my mind.

BOB

I can't look at Bob —
Not on the chain,
Not with the west wind
Blowin' the smell of fall on him,
And the coyotes on the ridge calling him,
And the stray dogs coming by, saying, "Come!"
See, Bob runs.
He was running one day with a pack of dogs.
I met them on the ridge, wild and high;
They had madness in their eyes:
Desperadoes, delinquents, off and dangerous —
"Bob!" I said.
And Bob came and stood by me,
Black and square;
Then the others turned away.
I told Bob's owner of course —
Now Bob is on the chain
And I walk the high ridges.

THE OLD WOLF

He was gray, yes gray,
Some black and some white,
Just enough shading
To fade in the night.
He had fur for the weather
And feet for the snow
And he drifted like smoke
Where he wanted to go.
His teeth were worn down
From the hard hunted bone,
He was shadowed by coyotes
He was never alone;
He was followed by ravens
By foxes and curs
And avoided the snares
And the trappers of furs.
His eyes they shone yellow
If caught in the light,
So he'd turn his big head
And look back at the night.
Of course he got careless,
All legends fail;
I saw him one evening
And shot the big male.
I took him to town,
Keith skinned him up right,
And he won't come a calling
On cattle at night,
And he won't come a calling
The wild in the wind . . .
So why do I feel
That somehow I sinned?
I cannot have timber wolves

Down by the herd,
And I once tried to tell him . . .
He heeded no word;
He heeded no warning,
He topped the food chain,
Or at least he still could
But for rifle and brain.

HANG

Hang!
Hang!
Hang on the wire;
Hang on the wire and dry.
You have chased my young calves,
And you've bothered my cows:
I've seen you go right for the eye!
You scoffed at my warnings,
So sure you could read the thoughts out of any man's head.
But I can lie deep, and I can shoot straight,
So now you are hanging there dead.
I dotted the fields near the place of the calving
With the bodies of all your black clan;
But you were so cocky, you always came back —
You thought you could match any man!
So hang on the wire, till you're feathers and air,
Hang till you're big beak and dust.
Then tell them in hell I can lie to the soul;
Tell them to take it on trust.
I roar at the wolves that come down in the dark,
And the ravens that come in the day.
I roar at the blackness, that this flesh is mine!
And I roared all your soaring away.
I am the keeper, and this is my fold:
Flare, when you come to the line.
Or hang on the wire, to tell all your type,
That everything, herein, is mine!

PRESERVED

A box of jam jars, all neatly arrayed
Wrapped in papers from home:
Pickles and compotes and jelly, preserves
Packed with the local tome.
News of the neighbours' visits,
Council, society fact,
Wrapped tight around the sealers
So they won't rattle and crack.
A nest not of twigs and grasses
Like the sparrow gleaner would use,
But a nest nonetheless
Her sister has made, a nest of the local news.
Pack it away in the trunk of the car,
Migrate back down to the south;
Food for the body, feed for the soul
And gathered up memory for mouth.
Can she feel the summer sun shining
Where the strawberries grew in the hay,
The scratch of the raspberry bushes
And the smell as they bubbled away?
She read of the weddings and funerals
With cucumber pickles, too tart;
She reads all the ads, how the harvest was bad,
And when the big cattle sale starts.
She eats apple jelly and wonders
What is written between the lines,
And her apartment alone smells like kitchens from home
With the sweet maple syrup so fine.
Does she sigh as she flattens the paper?
Does she smile as she puts it away?
Does she savor the joy of the chokecherry cloy
As red as a rain dawning day?
The sour sick smell of the city

Must fade, unable to fight,
When confronted with dilly bean pickles
And a paper from home in the night.

WINTER THUNDER

Oh it still likes to follow me
Everywhere I go:
Whippin' down for closing time
Or cruisin' really slow;
Walking round the pasture
Or plowing in the field,
Doing papers at the desk
To figure up the yield.
It follows me in summer,
It follows in the spring —
Like a thunderstorm in winter
It don't mean anything;
And it don't do nothing useful
'Cept whimper, plot and lie,
And make and break a promise
Saying, "Come on buddy try —
Come on; give it one more shot,
Come on, one more time."
Like a thunderstorm in winter,
Like an undiscovered crime,
Like as if I hadn't lots to do
Living soft and close and warm . . .
Without the curse of promise
Or a winter thunder storm.

SNOW

Snow, snow on the furrows and fields,
Snow where it used to be grain;
Snow in the beard, and snow in the eye,
Snowdrifts choking the lane.
Snow in the granary (from under the eaves),
Snow drifts up in the mow;
Snow in the stable, snow in the pen,
And wet snow under the cow.
Snow all clotting the coat of the mule
(The only thing out in the storm);
Snow in the evening, and snow in the night,
And snow from the west in the morn.
Drifted up snow as high as my head
Has hidden the fence post and rail;
Snow covered tracks where I walk to the barn,
And when I come back breakin' trail.
Snow in the air, and snow in the wind . . .
Snow, damn it, snow till ya bust.
Snow in the winter, and snow in the fall —
Snow in the spring if you must!
But sooner or later, I'll come digging out,
Out like a weed on a hill;
Snow all you want, I don't give a damn —
You do, and you always will.
Transient bastard! Your time is short:
Short as a cold winter day;
'Cause I bin around, to see lots like you —
And I know that you'll fail, about May.

THE WATCHER

I watched him, the way you watch a bull —
You know, the angle of the neck, the way he holds his head,
The eye — you have to watch the eye.
Say there's a cow in heat, and things around in the night
Squawking, yelping, eyes shining yellow . . .
You know how it is; he ain't never hurt you,
Never offered to; still, he is a bull.
That's how I watched him.
If a bull gets up sudden like,
You pay attention; you don't shine the light right on him,
Not when he stretches like that,
And he's been eating chop, and there are cows in heat all the
    time.
He's not a baby bull, a yearling or a two-year-old:
I'm talking about a ton of bone, balls and muscle —
Hell, he's been breeding thirty-five cows.
When he moves fast and clambers to his feet
You don't run, but you check the nearest fence.
Don't you dare act scared:
He must not know you're living at his whim;
He thinks he's living at yours —
Don't either of you forget that.

That's how I felt around him.
See he knew I had it all figured out —
I was on to him.
Partly bluff, but you never knew . . .
You never knew.

THE BARN

The big barn screamed like a beast in pain
As the dry-rotted timbers took the strain,
And the rusted nails pulled loose again
In the too familiar wind.
She shifted just a foot or two
And she screamed and groaned like lost ships do
As she slowly lost her lines so true —
Standing square and alone in the blast.
The crumbled concrete stable cracked,
The snow on her roof pushed down on her back,
The relentless wind wailed through the cracks
And the snow drift in the mow.
The hand-hewed hundred-year timbers bent,
And the new aluminum roofing went
And billowed and swelled like a flapping tent
When the pegs have pulled and gone.
The big barn sang her death song well,
And she sang it long before she fell,
For it's hard to break the "standing spell"
Of love and labour's hand.
Some planks flipped flew their long way down,
While her footings fought to hold the ground,
And the snow slid on her tortured crown
While the weary day wore on.
And no man heard her cry for aid
As she wailed for help like an outraged maid,
Except for those that long had laid
In their graves in the nearby hill.
And tears ran down from their hollow eyes
When they felt her splintering beauty die,
And they rolled the earth and gained the sky
As shadows in the wind.
They stood there mute in the howling gale,

And they saw her lean and they saw her fail,
While her cries ran up and down the scale —
Then the cruel north slapped her down.
The crash of her fall hid their cries of despair,
And the dust, hay and snow flew up in the air,
While broken timbers everywhere
Stuck up like ribs in the night.
The wind shrieked high in unholy glee
And smoothed her grave so the path was free,
And covered with drifts that "crafted tree"
Brought low by neglect and time.
The figures faded without a trace,
Except for one that held his place,
And the moonlight gleamed on his naked face . . .
His defiance damned the sky.
He ranted and railed in the face of God,
Then turned and crawled back in the sod,
In the grave on the hill where the wild wind trod
Its dervish dance of death.
So dreams die hard in Ontario
When the western gales so steady blow
And the land is six months under snow . . .
Mortality's at hand.

SOMETHING CALLING

Something calls from the rainy dark.
The blinds are open, a square of stark,
And out on the sodden April fields,
Something is looking in!
The idiot box is blaring,
Selling and telling lies.
While out in the dark and staring,
Something is lonely, and cries.
So I sit on the couch and listen,
With every fibre of me.
While my farm awakes, and it knows my name,
It's the fields that call to me.
It knows me deep, and I cannot hide:
It nags and it natters and calls —
It's got right hold of my blood and soul;
It can reach through distance and walls.
So I just sit here, and tremble,
Like a man in a trance or a spell,
While Freya wakens my thawing land,
And the call rings out like a bell.

THE LOVE AFFAIR

I can't quit it.
Even going down the road like this, with a business chore
    pressing,
I find myself checking Perry's cattle, Bob's cattle,
A pining cow, a limping steer, a lurking bear;
Scanning the edges for the deer,
Rushing home to write this thing, as if I hadn't hay to haul —
I can't quit it,
Never could, it was always like Mother Nature had her hand
    inside my pants.
I was not a good boy:
Never quiet, didn't get my homework done;
Trouble, trouble, all the time.
Oh, I tried;
Blew shifts in the mine — Oh God yes!
Turned new leaves a hundred times . . .
Couldn't quit it.
Quit the mine instead — now I farm:
Foolish farming, hunting's just a waste of time, and poetry . . .
I can't quit it.
Nature whispers in my ear and blows sweet breath on my face,
And I must grow and seek, participate and couple;
Someday she'll enfold me in her dark embrace
And show me things she's only hinted at before,
Squeeze my heart so hard it stops.
But until then,
I can't quit it.

Hunting

HAUNTED

I am haunted by marshes, by ridges and swales,
By hardwoods and edges, by funnels and trails,
By fallen down bridges, and roads through the back:
The canoe route, the portage, the old smoky shack,
The places we camped, and the places I shot,
The wind on the lake and the fire burned hot.
This farm may consume me and tie me up tight,
But I'm haunted by hunting, this time of the night.
On the mornings with frost, in the dusk with the dew,
When the coyotes are calling, I want to call too —
My rifle is handy, the wild's at the door,
I could go out stalking, where I've walked before;
It's just that the land has me hard at the heel,
And I can't go out worship the hot blood and steel.
But I'm haunted by places I've hunted before;
I dream of the tents of the camp on the shore . . .
The field's put to playing the song of the fall,
The meat in the freezer, the horns on the wall,
The wild way I wander, the wait, and the kill —
I'm haunted by hunting, and next week I will!

OFF

I'm off, I'm off, in the blowing snow
With my compass, map and rifle;
I don't know who will mind the farm,
But I hope my dog and wife'll.
I fed the cows to last two days;
It's wilder meat I'm after:
It's a drafty shack and a sleeping bag
In the bush, and manly laughter.
If they hide in the swamp we'll ferret them out,
If they browse on the hardwoods — stalk;
It's the half ton truck, a canoe in the muck,
And a good long sweaty walk.
It's the rifle report and the thump of the hit,
It's the raw red blood I'm shedding,
That draws me up to the stormy north
To sleep in soggy bedding.
It's the stories we'll tell as the fire smokes,
It's the booze and songs of sorrow;
My work that's left, I'll do when I can
And worry about tomorrow.

RIGHTS OF AUTUMN

Our coats all turn to fire
When the light is going down;
It's a mighty rite of autumn
Making meat out of the ground.
When the season turns to winter
You will find us cold and fey,
Everyone a shining beacon
At the closing of the day.
We bring death like gifts of wonder,
We take life out in the gray,
We fade in and out like whispers,
Then we silent slip away.
We are technologic predators
Singing songs as old as time,
As we join the waltz of winter
When the horned one's in his prime.
The ravens cheer and guide us
And the new men hate our way,
With our coats of fibre fire
At the closing of the day.

WITH A BUDDY, STILL HUNTING

He slammed the door on the half ton truck, "Is this where you
    want me now?"
I heard some crashing in the bush; it was just a frightened cow.
"Oh no," I whispered, "Let's just slip in. There's some rules in
    the brush."
"OK!" he bellowed lustily, and a distant partridge flushed.
He crushed a frozen puddle and he broke a deadfall down;
He coughed and swore and sputtered, as I spotted something
    brown.
It was halfway down the prairie and behind a cedar tree,
So I looked with my binoculars, and he said, "Whattaya see?"
I glassed the clearing edges, while he stomped his feet and
    talked;
"I don't see nothing here," he said. I whispered, "Let's just
    walk."
I started down the brushy edge as soft as I could go.
He said, "We won't get very far, you travel awful slow."
Just then a bunch of gunky does, in terror whitetailed by.
"Look at the deer! Look at the deer!" I heard my partner cry.
"Shut up for God's sake, there's no buck; he might just come
    behind."
I may have spoke too loudly, but I meant to, this one time.
I left him at the Poplar Point, and later shot a buck.
He helped me hang it in a tree, and said, "You sure have luck!
It's too bad I didn't get a shot; perhaps I will next year.
Let's wander back to camp," he said, "and grab ourselves a
    beer.
Oh, one more thing," he held his nose, "leave your jacket in
    the box.
You use so damn much cover scent, you smell just like a fox.
I don't know why we came this way, it's shorter from the
    south."
I could have pointed out the wind, but I just shut my mouth.

When they decided to make a drive, I only complained a bit,
'Cause they're so wise in the ways of the world, and I'm an
   ignorant hick.
And I must be insignificant; hell, I hardly scare the deer;
I just thanked my stars for all my luck, and had another beer.

TOTE ROAD DRIVE

We're hurlin' up the Tote Road
And we're throwin' her at curves;
She's belly bumpin' on the knolls,
Sprayin' gravel when she swerves.
We got beer bottles in our hands,
Our rifles on the rack;
We're goin' up to hunt for moose —
So far we're right on track.
We're slidin', spinnin', swervin'
Past the greenhorns on the trail;
At a hundred klicks and sometimes more
Just hear that tranny wail.
The canoe thinks it's a hurricane,
It's clingin' to the rack;
It's daylight in another hour —
So far we're right on track.
There's sod stuck in the wheel rims,
And brush caught in the grill,
'Cause it's third on every switch back,
And fourth for any hill.
The tires skip and stutter . . .
God help us coming back —
'Cause we've pushed our luck already;
Yes sir, we're right on track.
But does anybody whimper?
No sir, not one small whine:
'Cause we're sons of northern mothers
And so far we're doin' fine;
And just in case we're crazy
From starin' at the black
You best drive on your own side
'Cause so far we're right on track.

"FEARLESS HUNTER"

Perhaps you didn't hear me,
I was howlin' with my pack;
I missed the singing for a while,
I only just got back.
I was made and wrought a predator
With my eyes placed front and wise,
And I'm not too small to drag them down,
Nor too starvin' big in size.
I am designed for stamina,
For there's miles to hunt and run,
And I will kill more than I can eat —
For the future, call it fun.
I stand upright for a better view,
Or low if I must stalk,
And my feet are soft for sneaking,
And my legs are strong to walk.
I am really super at it
With my opposing thumbs and all,
So we had to limit when I hunt
To a week or so each fall.
But it's the function of my form,
The reason I am me;
So go eat tofu by yourself
And kindly let me be.

SILVER SILENCE

I sat in the bush by the edge of the field
While the silver dusk slid down;
The road it rattled over the ridge
Where the cars drove back to town.
The land got soft as a feather stroke,
And a sparrow gleaned away,
While a lonesome duck went frantically by,
And the light just slipped away.
No bear came out in the stubble field;
Perhaps it's just as well —
For a shot would disturb the hushing time
When the silver silence fell.
And when my sights were dim to see,
And every shadow — a bear,
I stood up soft and slipped away,
To leave the magic there.
Sometimes, you know, the best of hunts
Have no success at all . . .
Except to hear the hand of God
And the silver silence fall.

ROPES

Down by the lake the camps are vacant,
Unmarked snow by the door;
Up by the road the camps are empty,
Clean from the rafters to floor.
The old farmhouses show lightless windows,
The game pole ropes all sway,
The half ton trucks and the men with rifles
Have scattered — to worlds away.
The stands on the burns have ravens roosting,
The back trail ice is unbroke;
They're gone, they're gone, to the dream world waiting,
Back from the land awoke.
In the cedar groves the deer are stirring;
They're out in the fields again.
The half ton trucks and the men with rifles —
Not even their scent remains.
The cousins, the uncles, the nephews and brothers:
The clans have all scattered away,
And the camps and the cottages all stand empty —
The game pole ropes all sway.
The farmer goes out to endless choring:
To his cattle, their master, their slave —
Past the cottages, camps and the empty homesteads,
All quiet now as the grave.
And his kin in the south go back to the dreaming,
Back to the warm and the dry;
Back to the place where the soul is harnessed . . .
No need for the keen hunter's eye.
No need for the rifle, no need for the instinct,
No need for the camp by the lake —
The beast that is man slips back out of feeling;
The clan is no longer awake.
There is snow drifting deep on the trail to the cottage,

It is dark at the end of the day
And the coyotes snoop in cautious searching
Where the game pole ropes still sway.

Spirit

NAMER

Unless he walked on gravel
He made no sound at all;
He would harvest what he wanted
In the coming of the fall.
He could drift on in against the wind
And speak the wild goose call.

He could speak the language of the world
Be it wind or water; wail
The breeding call of moose or deer
Or the wolf's wild weirding tale.
He could read the land for the timber stand
Or the hidden portage trail.

Bulls would piss, the cougar hiss,
If they drew his downwind scent;
The women's wombs made feed and room
When he slept inside the tent.
The big bear bowed and gave him trail
And the fruit trees filled and bent.

He made his tools from the things at hand —
From the tree, from the rock, from the mind;
And he tamed the beasts to follow him,
And he tamed the fire to find,
And he fathered us every single one
And he named us as to kind.

He named us this, and he named us that,
And he placed us here and there
Wherever he traveled, wherever we dwelt

In the land of the lion or bear,
In the land of the tiger, the great gray wolf,
He gave his genetics to share.

Oh well, we call him diversified names
Or we worship, all in our own way;
In legends and stories, we sing of him too
In ballad, in dirge and in lay,
Or we try to forget him, and claim he's a dream
But he's printed, he won't go away.

Once in a time, or maybe again,
Maybe with dreams in his eyes,
He camps with the women and keeps them awake,
Then he travels to new lands and skies;
And he breeds so much in, that his blood is not thin,
And he quivers with each child that cries.

WANESA

She came up through the marsh where the hunters were
    camped,
Like a dream, she came alone —
She was fair, and as wet as a water lily
That the lake had chilled to the bone.
Their fire had smoldered just at dusk
From the rain in the foul east wind,
But the hunters jostled and made her room:
They snickered and blushed and grinned.
She said no word, though they questioned her,
But she smiled in a shy coy way,
And the embers in the fire died
As the night beat down the day.

They found them in their sleeping bags
When another gang came by;
They were cold and wet though the tent was good —
Experienced men to die!
And last week's weather wasn't that bad,
There was good food in the camp;
But every man was smiling and dead,
And every corpse was damp.

Somewhere up on the hardwood ridge
She wanders warm and fair,
As naked and slim as a poplar pole
With love knots in her hair.
Then every season will sap her strength
Till men camp near the marsh,
And she'll come to them to revive again
When the east wind's raw and harsh.

THE CURE

There are nine big lonely boulders
Where the alder swamp plays out.
A trap trail crosses on the marsh,
There, or there about.
There's an elemental presence
That they call a Wendigo . . .
And even beasts go wide around —
There are no tracks on the snow.

Madness overtook him,
Somewhere on the trail,
And had man or God been listening,
They'd have heard that poor soul wail;
But only forest darkness
Saw him sit and grab his face,
When the rabies finally caught him —
He was frozen in his place.
He ground his teeth in fury,
And he broke the last wall down,
Like he smashed the rotten alders,
As he thrashed upon the ground.
The bull moose pissed in terror,
And the wild wolf fled in fright,
While he bit his frothing lips and screamed,
Somewhere in the night.
The breath that God breathed in him
Was steaming on the air.
Neither God nor man was listening —
There was only madness there.
He was howling, raving, shrieking,
Like a beast. Lost in the Fog.
He split his teeth in fury,
And he bayed like a running dog.

His spirit fled in horror,
And something felt it go.
It had dwelt in sleeping apathy;
Now it woke to see the show.
Like northern lights it flickered
On his hair-raised, twitching form;
While his soul watched on in wonder,
A compound thing was born.
It climbed up cut and frothy,
And its arms hung by its side;
Its eyes unfocused, glassy,
And its wrecked mouth gaping wide.
Then it flung its arms out tautly,
And it screamed like none before —
The nesting geese on the far lake side,
Flew night bound from the shore.
Its throat worked like a crawling snake,
And it roared out yet again . . .
The virus left the body,
And the Wendigo the brain.
The spirit drifted in again,
And the thing became a man,
While the northern lights danced through the night
Like a waving ethereal hand.

There are nine big lonely boulders
Where the alder swamp plays out.
A trap trail crosses on the marsh,
There, or there about.
It's always been an eerie place,
Where you never stop to rest.
It's touched many things, in its long long sleep,
But that cool May night was best.

THE CHALLENGE

I dreamed one night of the young red cow
Down, in a gully crotch;
There was something there, a challenge, a dare
In the foggy glass I watch —
I saw in the vision a broken hoof
Where the muddy water seeps,
And I said to myself, "It's because I'm lame,
But this gives me the creeps."
And "Hoven, Hoven Gurry our foe,"
Was always on my mind,
For it is the song I never sing
Without death among the kine.
And I saw her calf, among the herd,
Go gaunt and go alone,
For the young red cow with the cripply feet
Was never a comin' home.
So when I was well, and could hobble along,
I went where I thought I saw . . .
But that gully was empty of any dead sign,
With only green grass in the draw.
I elbowed my gun and I rolled me a smoke
And I thought on the lay of the land,
For there is another spot like that
Not too far out of hand.
So I limped along to Heffeller creek
Where the tagalders drain to the south,
And there in the grass, by the water like glass,
Lay the bones of my cow, by the mouth.
The round hills swelled like they had in the dream
And her bones were scattered a lie,
And a broken hoof was jammed in tight —
In the skull, in the hole for the eye.
Jammed in tight, I could not get it free:

A talisman, curse, or a dare;
The exact cause of death was hard to explain,
Though she was fed on by wolf and by bear.
But what was the power that snatched her away
When she cried out to me, in my sleep?
Or was it the power that nudged me awake
Then shuffled away to its keep?
For never an animal drove in that toe,
Lodging it solid to see.
A force in the wilderness, savage as time
Had issued a challenge to me —
I take and I harvest, I hunt and I graze,
I live as if outside The Law;
So it could be that nature just harvested back
In the fall, by the mouth of the draw.

PREDATOR

Willow nets we spun for him,
Web as fine and strong as fate;
Spells we cast, upon the last,
Upon the loom, and on the weight.
Mares tails wound we in, while spinning,
Washed in water from the bog;
Dream trails wound we in the weaving,
Grass we burned into the fog.

Never were our snares confronted
Though the effigies were hung;
And we found no spoor of passing —
Neither track, or hair, or dung.

Steel we forged, our hammers thundered,
Ore we stole from out the hill,
Traps with jaws of jutted iron,
Plans we plotted, brain and will;
Electronic circuits soldered,
One and zero intertwine,
Thoughts, a thousand in a heartbeat —
Invisible our hook and line.

But never, never, not one moment,
Neither dung, nor track, nor hair . . .
And if he didn't feed so often,
We would say he wasn't there.

MASTER OF THE FIVE F's

I have learned to control it:
The lift in the chest,
The humming of the heart,
The narrowing of vision,
The sweaty palms . . .
I don't like it;
It clouds the mind,
Leads to missed opportunities,
Tragedy, tears, disappointment,
Indigestion —
And early death.
There is an atavistic magic in it:
Spells of ancestors,
Masters of the five F's.
It doesn't lend itself to harness —
Analytical thought, and precision of enterprise —
But to red hazed madness,
Passion, and unholy oaths.
When the dark is down, and the prey might fight,
The dog might bite, and the plane might light
Unexpectedly,
It doesn't help to lose control.
That hairy little mad man in your blood
Is seldom of assistance;
He gets caught in the gears of our mechanism
And drags us in as well.
Chain him, or he'll bury you.

THE SACRIFICE

Billy built a pyre, on the looming far land hill,
But before he lit the fire, he brought a bull to kill;
Halter broke and pedigreed, he led him up the slope,
Clean of line, and quiet, fine, he never fought the rope.
Beneath the sky dark scudding clouds, Billy spoke to God,
While down below, in tended row, his land stretched rod on
    rod;
Now Billy spoke in silence, while the rolling sky went over,
And he knelt bare headed on the hill, on pastured regrowth
    clover.
He knew his God, his God knew him, an ancient pact and
    plan —
His elder God, in thunder trod, and the earth's hard tending
    man.
He offered up in sacrifice, the best he had to give,
And he prayed in still petition that his only son would live;
The blow he struck, the blood he shed, the smoke climbed to
    the sky,
Reached someone ancient waiting: the Answer and the Why.
Can you give a name to power, give a title to the Word?
Atavistic and unorthodox, Billy's prayer was heard.
Was it drugs and modern medicine? A triumph of the will?
No! The cure was God and Billy, and the bull he brought to
    kill.

WEBBWOOD

The gravestones, neat, erect and cold,
Stand in Webbwood's graveyard, under the overpass.
Under the March rain and rotting drifts.
Under a little lake of icy water,
Over the graves . . .
In the graves?
Silent waves of clammy clay
Caress the corpses.
Why do I care?
The dead don't care;
Only the living on the overpass,
Speeding glibly by,
Look and shudder at Webbwood's graves.
And Webbwood's wells,
Are they bitter in the spring?
Do weeping, worried woes seep in,
And gibbering memories in your glass?
While drinking morning coffee . . .

    "Remember poor old What's His Name
    Who used to live just down the lane?
    I wonder why I thought of him
    On such a dreary morning."

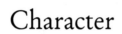

Character

HELL'S VIEW

I was raised on a hill at Hell's Corner,
We hardly saw law there at all;
And I still watch the door when I'm resting,
And sit with my back to the wall.
I can see the side road from my kitchen,
I keep weapons scattered around,
I got scars, some that ain't showing —
Don't ever let me get you down.
I was raised by a tough little mad man
In a place just outside of the fold;
I don't compromise what I'm thinking,
And even when angry I'm cold.
See, you read what I'm writing and rhyming
And you think that I'm one way; I'm not.
I was raised on a hill at Hell's Corner —
You learn pretty fast in that spot.
You learn how to sharpen and carry,
You learn how to shoot, or you will;
It's a rough little spot is Hell's Corner,
When viewed from the edge of the hill.
A paranoid view is a virtue
If the aim of the world, is your end,
Or even your modification
When you're too God damned stubborn to bend.

TRIUMVIRATE

When we sit in solemn conference,
Just we sacred three,
We solve the problems of the world —
Steve and Pete and me.
We all come at it different ways;
It has no place to hide,
And if it burrows under rock
We mine it from inside.
We burn it in the fire,
We build it into form,
We flesh it out from inside out,
So different we were born.
We live, by Christ, so close at hand
It's Gibson's when we're dry;
I never saw a problem
That we three weren't prone to try.
And if Steve and I don't know it
Pete will break the track,
And if Pete and I don't know the thing
Then Steve will set it back.
I ain't that smart at stuff like that
But once in just a while
We hit something they can't figure —
I solve it with a smile.
I solve it, or he handles that,
Or we all jump for joy;
Just give us half a reason
And a season for a toy.
Just sit right back and watch the smoke,
Have a smoke for free;
A fat forty pounder (Gibson's),
And Pete and Steve and me.

THE JAWS

I used to drive the back roads hard,
As if I were holding my courage and my skill
Tight against the gravel,
My wealth to burn: in trucks, in gas, in shocks and rubber —
Skipping on the sliding stones
As if upon that belly rush of speed.
Oh, I have mellowed much . . .
Now my stately progress hardly raises dust.
No one wonders if I want to race:
"Who is that," they probably say,
"Gray in the mirror?
What defeat has tested him, and stolen the joy of dizzy speed?"
I'll tell you:
Time, and that sad and certain knowledge
Of the law; the law of men and nature stalks me now
And watches for a misstep like a wolf.
And like an old beast in the field
I go without display — to draw attention
Is to slide into the jaws.

PROMISE

Ah, what can I say,
My light of the heart,
That has not been said before?
On what can I swear, with what compare,
That has not been claimed on more?
Can I speak of the way my cold heart jumps,
Of the way my longing aches?
Should I speak in allusion, or metaphor:
Fire and wind and lakes?
What are we but flesh that carries a soul —
Beasts once breathed awake,
With only a moment to pass on the light,
With only a promise to take.
Oh, what can I promise
My twinkling jewel?
Not youth, though it's ours for a time.
And never forever, forever is not —
We are locked in the metre and rhyme;
We are locked in the dance
And the dance must go on,
Generations behind and to be . . .
I promise the future, the future to come,
Dancing with you and with me.

EXPLANATION

I never have done nothing wrong;
I never broke the law.
Well . . . I poached a deer, when just a boy
Down in my Daddy's draw;
But the freezer it was empty
And Dad had broke his leg
And we never were on welfare
And we never liked to beg.
Oh, I took a crescent wrench with me
When I worked in the mine;
But everybody pilfered stuff —
It seemed right at the time.
And there's little stuff, like seat belt laws,
I broke a time or two;
But I never did do anything
That I won't admit to you.
Oh sure, I fought with fists, and hard,
Two times — maybe three;
But the other fellows started it,
And would have waled on me.
I have profaned, and several times
I have lusted, I admit it.
And I have been mad and full of hate,
But I always could forget it.
So here I stand before you
With this shotgun in my hand:
I've killed myself; I've killed my wife;
I also shot the man.
I know just where I'm going
Be it down or hell or south,
And I also knew your judgment
When I put it in my mouth.
I have nothing I can say

To make it look all right . . .
But it twisted up my guts so hard,
I was driven to this night —
I was driven like a goaded bull,
By betrayal, by the beast;
And I can't say I'm repentant —
I can tell the truth at least.
I stand in pain before you
With this shotgun in my hand,
And I say I'd do it all again —
My wife, my self, the man.

THE PLOT

Oh, you can kiss a shotgun, to try to ease the pain,
But you can't cheat your redemption,
And you'll do it all again.
Like a poorly written novel, or a movie with no plot,
You'll live it all, all over —
You can't end it with a shot.
You can't flip through to the ending; you can't hear the
    punchline first;
You can't drain the bitter dregs
Before you quench your thirst.
I don't offer explanations, and I didn't write your tale,
So don't expect apologies —
Just walk the whole damn trail.
It is you must bear the burden; it is you must climb the hill,
It is your fate, and you must wait,
It's not your time to kill.
And if it all seems pointless, it's been pointless once before;
But you'll have to watch and wonder
What new plot twist lies in store.
You can hurry up the ending, but you can't hide in the night;
So you'll simply have to work on it:
This time, get it right.

NOT DEPRESSION

I see seven boarded businesses
From the barber shop front door,
And the train that ain't the CPR
Don't stop here anymore;
It rolls right through, 'bout twice a day,
Highway 17 is light,
So there is no service station now
That's open here at night.
There ain't but eight old farmers,
And when they up and die
There'll be brush upon the front road fields
You'll see when you go by.
You'll see our sign, beside the road,
Our sons with waiting pack,
Hitchhiking somewhere down the line —
Those boys aren't coming back.
Oh, where's it gone the miner's dream?
To miner's lung and curse.
To slashes up the Tote Road; still
The loggers left here first —
The loggers left, the farmers died,
The miners moved away.
Now the last old rubbies ask again,
"A dollar?" Not today.
There's a dozen rusty pickups
At the remaining coffee shop;
We can use the stimulation
And we've lots of time to stop.

KIMBERLITE KEN

The weather doesn't like us here, but this old land likes men;
Like a Grandma with a cookie jar it tempts us, guys like Ken.
It lured his native blood with passage, a system wet and loose:
With fish and foul and furs to wear, deer and bear and moose.
His white part portaged in for pine, and stayed for fertile land,
And they bore the bitter weather, 'cause this hard land likes
    man.

Ken, he was a ne'er-do-well, he'd tell you so himself;
He had no drive or ambition; he'd purchase off the shelf:
The easy way, the common way, work clothes — green or tan,
Country music, half ton trucks, a draught beer drinking man.
A single guy, a part-time sort, you see them all around;
I could name a half a dozen in any northern town.
Ken failed at fruit stands, farming, and at pumping gas and life,
And I think I heard a rumor, he was married — lost his wife;
Ken even screwed up welfare; I don't understand the whole:
He forgot to do some paper work, and was off the pogey roll.

Now, Ken was getting on a bit, his bridges burned behind,
And you can bet, in a place like this, he had shelter on his
    mind:
Somewhere to put a garden, in some hollow for a shack,
Perhaps a lake with pickerel and a moose or two out back.
See Ken had dropped the bullshit off, each time he dropped a
    rung,
And all he had was in his head, a canoe, some books, a gun,
A rusty racky S 10 truck, some ragged clothes and tools —
But there's room up here for dreamers, for failures and for
    fools.
You can't just squat upon the land like his grandpa used to do
Unless you make a prospect claim, and that's what Ken would
    do.

He bought a license (fifty bucks); he made a claim, same day,
And he loaded up his half-ton truck, and Ken he drove away.

He built a one-room shotgun shack beside a little lake
Where the land had lots to offer . . . and Ken began to take.
He had to cut the strips around, "Run the God damned lines,"
But he only wanted to live up there; he had worked in a mine,
So Ken he knew a little about minerals and ore,
And he had a *Northern Miner*, from his last trip to the store.
He bought it for the articles, but he read it all day long,
So he had a rough idea exploration was going strong.
It didn't amaze him, not at all, to see drill trucks go by;
And he bought the boys a coffee, if they stopped, or just
    waved "Hi."

Ken got a job that summer as a fishing guide and cook;
He'd show them where to cast and troll, take the muskies off
   - the hook.
He'd drink their beer and whisky, and listen to them talk,
Their bragging and their bullshit — then he'd take them for a
   walk
And they'd fish for rapids' speckles, and they'd fish for back
   pond bass;
It was just the kind of job for Ken — sitting on his ass.

But when Ken returned one evening, there were new trucks
   by his shack,
And a bunch of balding burly men, were walking round out
   back;
It didn't bother Ken at all, he could read the half ton doors
And he knew the emblem written there: those boys were
   from DE BOERS.

So Ken he got a lawyer, and he signed off in the end —
The weather here's against us, but this hard land is a friend:
It tempted man with copper, until copper didn't pay;
It tried nickel, gold and silver, but we squandered that away;
It produced boxite, iron, platinum, uranium and stuff,
Till it had to pipe up diamonds, for our diamond in the rough.

Now Ken's the guided rich guy, and Ken's the widow's joy,
And a fellow who'd ignored him, now claims to be his boy;
But Ken just drinks draught in the bar like any other man,
And he still wears work clothes every day: blue or green or
     tan.

THE TURNING

When the good earth enfolds me,
Or the bright flames consume me,
Or the water shall wash me away —
I shall be recycled, eventually cycled,
And I will awake in a day.

I would if allowed be eaten by eagles,
By ravens and crows and their kin;
Then I'd look from their feathers, aloft and asoaring,
I'd look from their feathers and grin.

This body's the shell that has carried my spirit;
It bore it both lively and well.
So when I don't need it, I don't want to greed it . . .
Let nature just turn it a spell.

The Line in the Sand

JOHN SMITH (OR TRANSLATION)

In a hole close to Ypres I was gassed and then shot;
When I stood up to breathe I was killed on the spot.
I was part of a trench just left there to rot
With the rest of the men and the garbage.

I screamed on a bayonet, Culloden Moor;
I crawled off to die, but they followed the spoor.
There was no thought of mercy, parole for the poor —
I was shot like a dog, in the morning.

A great big barbarian broke in my head,
Then tore out my lungs, and left me there dead.
I don't know the place, but the earth it was red
As it dripped in my face in the evening.

I followed the banner the wild world across:
The eagle, the crescent, the yak tail, the cross —
And in every damn battle I was the loss
Regardless who camped in the carnage.

Now the bugle is blowing, the drums start to beat,
My blood it is rolling, my body's the meat.
I am called to the slaughter; I can't rule my feet —
My destiny's soaked in the music.

So bring on the paper, the preacher, the priest;
I am the flesh that hungers the beast.
Of all of the sacrifice, mine is the least . . .
I'm just part of the list, in my passing.

THE SAFETY FASCIST

He was neatly coifed (as far as I noticed),
A conservative suit (as much as I saw),
And he spoke of duty, to protect us, for safety,
While my eyes were locked just under his jaw.
His voice was as smooth as an old adder's belly;
His words were as soothing as a rain ended day;
But I didn't listen, I watched fascinated
The spot on his throat where the ear grew away.
He waved his soft hands (the nails, they were polished);
He was keen on his point: preservation of life;
How he'd make the streets safe if he took all our weapons —
I was two feet away and I fingered the knife
Folded there in my pocket, as sharp as a razor,
Three inches long, two inches to spare . . .
While he went on in logic about the need for protection,
And I just walked away — not me, and not there.
There were sharp shards of glass on the glistening sidewalk,
A stout bar of iron leaned on the wall,
And my hands are strong . . . but my leash is convention —
Still, life is so fragile: my weapon is all.

A HUNDRED THOUSAND HEADS

There's a problem with democracy, bureaucracy and fools,
For the fops the freaks and frightened folks
Are making all the rules.
It would be nearly funny; it could make a cynic smile,
But they're mucking with the gears of life —
They have been quite a while.
See it all worked to perfection when most men were on the
    land,
And the women taught and nurtured,
And the kids were under hand.
But it all got twisted up a bit with red tape everywhere,
And they've slipped their pale soft fingers
Right inside our underwear.
They do not care for common sense — they've got us by the
    balls,
And our hearts and minds will follow,
And we'll answer when they call.
You can't argue with them (reason); you can't hope they'll go
    away —
The insane run the asylum;
You can bet they plan to stay.
They don't understand plain language, they don't listen, they
    don't care —
They just twist the red tape fingers
Deep inside our underwear.
What can we do about it? I'm leaving that to you;
I am just another simple voice
That doesn't have a clue.
Perhaps we need a Robespierre — a Marat — or a King . . .
When he comes, by Christ, we'll listen
Or we're not worth anything.

WHERE THERE'S SMOKE

The allegations held some truth —
Rumors often do;
And no one mortal's perfect:
Neither he, or me, or you.
No one I can think of
Never fornicated, lied,
Never squandered, stole, or slandered,
Beat a weaker man or tried.
Oh we poached and pooled our permits,
Broke the small stuff on the list;
We are human beings after all,
Just beasts that God has kissed.
We are all of us judgmental,
Listing flaws our brothers bear,
While we bumble on in tragedy
Pretending that we care —
Pretending that our souls are pure
We rationalize our sin
While we whisper to our fellows
"There's a villain — look at him."

TIP

It was not so much the betrayal,
I have been betrayed before,
I've been informed on, lied to and about,
Suckered and knocked to the floor;
But I just can't come to expect it,
And each time it cuts like a saw,
Then I heal and crust over my anger
And pretend that the wound is not raw.
See, the folks who really can hurt you
Are the ones who are close and can reach.
The law, though the law it is mighty,
Can only fine, jail and impeach.
Oh the Law, I know that we need it;
The law, like a fire we must cross —
The constables, cops, with their flat black props,
And only free will is the loss.
And I don't mind that they are so watchful --
Or I do, but I take it in stride —
But it's those God Damned rats with their secretive chats
That can get me to fester inside.
See, either they do it for money,
Their Judas coins secret and slick,
Or they do it to make the world better . . .
The thought of that makes me feel sick.
What kind of world are they wanting,
To inform on their neighbors and friends?
What kind of twisted redemption
Makes that seem right in the end?
How do you look in the mirror?
Do you flinch when you come to the eye?
Or do you pretend as you squeal out a friend
It's your duty to not tell a lie?
It's your duty to make the world better —

You sanctimonious fool!
And even the lawmen don't like you:
You're a dirty despicable tool.
And what kind of tool must be hidden?
One that works to tear us apart —
The harm that you are, is a pus-seeping scar,
But you must have known that from the start.
And that's why you rat out your comrades;
In secret you're small and alone,
But the damage you do, is greater than you:
You infect us all to the bone.

THE TAKING

I can remember as clear as a bell
What I always wanted to be:
A father, a farmer, a good rifle shot —
And that's what I got. It is me.
I wanted a truck and a tractor and land,
I wanted some cattle to feed;
But I didn't want trouble, or politics games —
I had little ambition or greed.
I was always a poet, my people before,
I wanted some learning to write;
And I wanted some grandkids close to the end
To warm my name into the night.
I wanted to farm, and I wanted to hunt,
I wanted some friends and a drink;
I wanted tobacco, sugar, and salt —
And what else? Just let me think . . .
I wanted to be left alone on my land
In the place of my parents before.
I wanted my rights, God damn it, my rights:
It was freedom that I wanted more;
The freedom to be what I wanted to be —
I wanted the world as my friend.
But the world's turned against me, I cannot fight back,
And you're taking it all, in the end.
What did I ever do to you folks
That you hound me from pillar to post;
I never hurt anyone, I can recall,
But you're taking the things I love most.
You are taking my life, one law at a time,
You, and your rules of today . . .
There's no Medicine Line I can cross to escape,
As you legislate my life away.

BIOGRAPHY

Charlie Smith was born in Blind River, Ontario in 1948. His mother Iona Hamilton of Spanish, Ontario wrote poetry, as did her father Charlie Hamilton, also of Spanish. Charlie's father, Charles T. Smith was from Illinois, and Charlie was "shook round this continent / Like a pebble in a can," attending public school in Silver Water, Ont., Rockford, Ill., Elizabeth Bay, Ont., Grand Detour, Ill., Spanish, Ont., Grand Detour, Ill. (again), and Evansville, Ont. He went to High School in Orangeville, Ont., and Gore Bay, Ont., where he graduated with his grade 12 diploma. He married his wife Rhonda Lane just out of high school, and spent 10 years in the INCO mines in Sudbury. He and Rhonda then bought their home — christened Earthfast — on the Birch Lake Road, northeast of Massey, Ont., where Charlie fulfilled his dream of being "A father, a farmer, a good rifle shot." They have three children, Rebecca, Chuck, and Brandon, and recently have become grandparents, to Maeve.